EVERY 小 小 的 幸福
DAY
Is a FUN DAY

by
Andrea Voon

illustrated by
Yapp Shin Enn

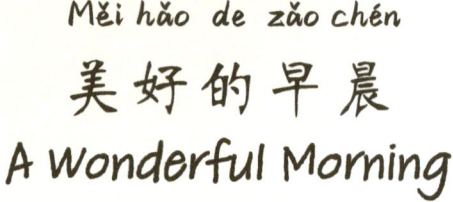

Měi hǎo de zǎo chén
美好的早晨
A Wonderful Morning

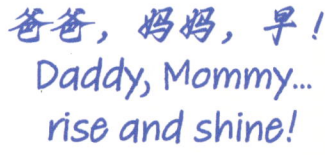

爸爸，妈妈，早！
Daddy, Mommy...
rise and shine!

The sun is smiling. The birds are singing.
What shall we do today? Where shall we go today?
The time is ticking and we can't stay!
Let's go outside, so we can play...

1

Chuāng wài tài yáng nuǎn nuǎn zhào　lán tiān　bái yún yě zài xiào
窗外太阳暖暖照，蓝天、白云也在笑，

niǎo ér huān xǐ de chuī kǒu shào　qī pàn de zhōu mò yǐ lái dào
鸟儿欢喜地吹口哨，期盼的周末已来到。

Xiǎo xiǎo de xìng fú　yǒu nǐ men péi zhe qù xún zhǎo
小小的幸福，有你们陪着去寻找！

Xiǎo xiǎo de xìng fú　yǒu nǐ men péi zhe qù xún zhǎo
小小的幸福，有你们陪着去探讨！

野餐踏青
Day Out

Jiāo yóu dài shàng dà bāo xiǎo bāo   zì xíng chē qí shàng xiū xián dào
郊游带上大包小包，自行车骑上休闲道，

pù hǎo cān diàn máng duī shā bǎo   cǎo dì yě cān yě wèi kǒu hǎo
铺好餐垫忙堆沙堡，草地野餐也胃口好。

Wǒ de hǎo lǎo shī   wèi shé me fēng zheng zǒng shì wǎng xià diào
我的好老师，为什么风筝总是往下掉？

Wǒ de hǎo lǎo shī   wǒ de fēng zhēng zhōng yú fēi shàng le yún xiāo
我的好老师，我的风筝终于飞上了云霄。

Family outing is **fun** with you as my great teacher.

Let's pack a picnic, and feel the love of nature.

Sandy beach, deep blue sea... The castle stands upright.

Singing birds, fresh green grass... Our little kites take flight.

Dēng shān yuǎn zú

登山远足
Into the Woods

Gǔ shù cān tiān lù yè mào   bó wù huán rào zhe shān yāo
古树参天绿叶茂，薄雾环绕着山腰，

chǎng bái pù bù shēng tāo tāo   fǔ shǒu dà dì de měi mào
长白瀑布声涛涛，俯首大地的美貌。

Qīn ài de hù lín yuán   xiǎo dòng wù kě xǐ huān wán duǒ māo māo
亲爱的护林员，小动物可喜欢玩躲猫猫？

Qīn ài de hù lín yuán   xiǎo dòng wù dōu biǎo xiàn de hǎo hài sào
亲爱的护林员，小动物都表现得好害臊。

Hiking is **fun** with you as my park ranger.

Let's dive into the woods, and spot the friendliest creature.

Dangling vines, thick tree branches, the leafy stems say, "HI!"

Shimmering streams, thundering falls, the frogs and fish are shy!

Xiǎo xiǎo yùn dòng yuán

小小运动员
Little Athlete

Diǎn dian tóu   wān wan yāo   shēn shen shǒu   dēng deng jiǎo
点点头，弯弯腰，伸伸手，蹬蹬脚。
Dài shàng fú quān shuǐ shang piāo   wò jǐn qiú gǎn bīng shang sǎo
戴上浮圈水上漂；握紧球杆冰上扫。
Qīn ài de duì zhǎng   xiǎo xiǎo de lóng mén kě shǒu de láo
亲爱的队长，小小的龙门可守得牢？
Qīn ài de duì zhǎng   xiè xie nǐ wèi wǒ hǎn jiā yóu kǒu hào
亲爱的队长，谢谢你为我喊加油口号。

Sport training is **fun** with you as my team leader.

Let's warm up your muscles, and practice together.

Paddle, paddle, kick... I can be a good swimmer;

Dribble, dribble, shoot... I can beat the goalkeeper.

咕......咕咕!
Ho...ot! Hoot!

Yě wài lù yíng

野外露营
Camping

Zhàng péng dā de yào láo kào　　shēng qǐ yíng huǒ ruǎn táng kǎo
帐篷搭得要牢靠, 生起营火软糖烤。

cháo luò shǒu qiān shǒu qù xún bǎo　　cháo qǐ nài xīn děng yú shàng diào
潮落手牵手去寻宝; 潮起耐心等鱼上钓。

Qīn ài de tóng jūn　　māo tóu yīng wèi hé hái bù shuì jiào
亲爱的童军, 猫头鹰为何还不睡觉?

Qīn ài de tóng jūn　　wǒ tīng jiàn le kǒng bù de láng háo
亲爱的童军, 我听见了恐怖的狼嚎。

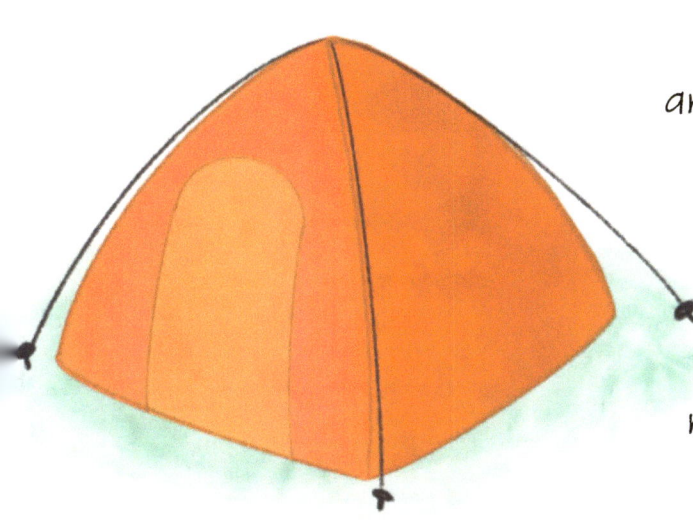

Camping is **fun** with you as my scout and guide.

Let's build a campfire,
and the marshmallows will roast.

Hunting at low tide;
fishing at high tide.

And best of all --
Staying out all night,
make our bed by the riverside!

行万里路
Xíng wàn lǐ lù

Traveling

Dǎ kāi dì tú huà shàng zuò biāo
打开地图画上坐标，

nǐ dìng jià rì de xíng chéng biǎo
拟定假日的行程表。

Chuān le jiù shēng yī dài yǎn zhào
穿了救生衣戴眼罩，

hǎi shang fú qián zì zài xiāo yáo
海上浮潜自在逍遥。

Qīn ài de huǒ bàn
亲爱的伙伴，

dà hǎi li yǒu shé me xī qí zhū bǎo
大海里有什么稀奇珠宝？

Qīn ài de huǒ bàn
亲爱的伙伴，

zhè shì hǎi yáng zhī bǎo
这是海洋之宝——

shān hú jiāo
珊瑚礁。

Traveling is **fun** with you as my companion.

Let's open the map, and plan a special vacation.

HOORAY! we're taking a boat to our destination.

QUICK! we're ready to explore the beautiful ocean!

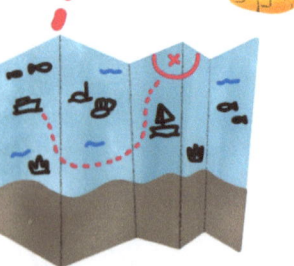

Wán zhuǎn yóu lè yuán

玩转游乐园
Playground

Gōng yuán zhuī zhú bǐ sài pǎo　　qiū qiān dàng de bǐ tiān gāo
公园追逐比赛跑，秋千荡得比天高，

jīn zì tǎ gōng dǐng kǎo jì qiǎo　　xuán zhuǎn huá tī nàn bu dǎo
金字塔攻顶考技巧，旋转滑梯难不倒。

Qīn ài de bǎo biāo　　jiē shi de jiān bǎng kě fǒu ràng wǒ kào
亲爱的保镖，结实的肩膀可否让我靠？

Qīn ài de bǎo biāo　　shì wǒ men xìng fú de yī kào
亲爱的保镖，是我们幸福的依靠。

Playtime is **fun** with you as my protector.

Let's reach for the sky, or try the cup spinner.

Climb up the pyramid; Spiral down the slide.

Until we hear, "Five more minutes,

it's time for a piggyback ride."

14

充实的一天
Chōng shí de yì tiān

A Fruitful Day

Jiā wù láo zuò bìng bù wú liáo　　shōu shí wán jù　　bāng máng dǎ sǎo
家务劳作并不无聊，收拾玩具，帮忙打扫；

Yuè dú tiān dì shēn cáng ào miào　　rèn zhēn xué xí　　xì xīn tǎo jiào
阅读天地深藏奥妙，认真学习，细心讨教。

Qīn ài de mā ma　　gù shì de jié jú kě fǒu jiē xiǎo
亲爱的妈妈，故事的结局可否揭晓？

Qīn ài de mā ma　　wǒ men yǒu sì zhāng dòng wù yuán mén piào
亲爱的妈妈，我们有四张动物园门票。

Cleaning is **fun** with you as my best partner.

Let's grab a mop or broom,

and tidy up the family room;

Reading is fun with you as my storyteller.

Let's share a book or two,

and earn some tickets to the zoo.

Chāo rén bà ba

超人爸爸
Superdaddy

Fàng xià gōng shì bāo hé diàn nǎo   tǎo gè xiāng wěn hé yōng bào

放下公事包和电脑，讨个香吻和拥抱。

Zuǒ yòu   zuǒ yòu shì bīng bù cāo   yī èr   yī èr mǎ er màn pǎo

左右、左右士兵步操；一二、一二马儿慢跑。

Qīn ài de bà ba   gōng zuò le yī tiān kě jué pí láo

亲爱的爸爸，工作了一天可觉疲劳？

Qīn ài de bà ba   lǎo shī zàn wǒ shì gè guāi bǎo bao

亲爱的爸爸，老师赞我是个乖宝宝。

Bonding time is **fun** with you as my best buddy.

A kiss and a hug can boost your super energy.

LEFT…LEFT…LEFT…RIGHT…LEFT…

Here comes the army;

GIDDY-UP! GIDDY-UP! GIDDY-UP-UP-UP…

There goes the pony.

美梦甜甜
Sweet Dream

Yuè er pá shang le shù shāo　xīng xing zuān jin le mián ǎo
月儿爬上了树梢，星星钻进了棉袄。

Zhěn tou zhàn luàn le chuáng jiǎo　dǎ dǎo dí rén hù chéng bǎo
枕头战乱了床角，打倒敌人护城堡。

Qīn ài de mèi mei　shuì mèng li zěn me hái zài xiào
亲爱的妹妹，睡梦里怎么还在笑？

Qīn ài de mèi mei　zhù nǐ měi mèng tián tián dào qīng zǎo
亲爱的妹妹，祝你美梦甜甜到清早。

Bedtime is **fun** with you as my royal knight.

Let's protect the queen, and start the pillow fight.

Big bad wolf is dead, it's time to say goodnight.

The moon and the stars will shine through the night.

20

<ruby>严<rt>Yán</rt></ruby> <ruby>厉<rt>lì</rt></ruby> <ruby>的<rt>de</rt></ruby> <ruby>爸<rt>bà</rt></ruby> <ruby>爸<rt>ba</rt></ruby>， <ruby>稳<rt>wěn</rt></ruby> <ruby>重<rt>zhòng</rt></ruby> <ruby>又<rt>yòu</rt></ruby> <ruby>可<rt>kě</rt></ruby> <ruby>靠<rt>kào</rt></ruby>； <ruby>温<rt>Wēn</rt></ruby> <ruby>柔<rt>róu</rt></ruby> <ruby>的<rt>de</rt></ruby> <ruby>妈<rt>mā</rt></ruby> <ruby>妈<rt>ma</rt></ruby>， <ruby>心<rt>xīn</rt></ruby> <ruby>灵<rt>líng</rt></ruby> <ruby>又<rt>yòu</rt></ruby> <ruby>手<rt>shǒu</rt></ruby> <ruby>巧<rt>qiǎo</rt></ruby>。

<ruby>姐<rt>Jiě</rt></ruby> <ruby>姐<rt>jie</rt></ruby> <ruby>和<rt>hé</rt></ruby> <ruby>妹<rt>mèi</rt></ruby> <ruby>妹<rt>mei</rt></ruby>， <ruby>活<rt>huó</rt></ruby> <ruby>泼<rt>pō</rt></ruby> <ruby>爱<rt>ài</rt></ruby> <ruby>撒<rt>sā</rt></ruby> <ruby>娇<rt>jiāo</rt></ruby>， <ruby>一<rt>yí</rt></ruby> <ruby>会<rt>huì</rt></ruby> <ruby>儿<rt>er</rt></ruby> <ruby>争<rt>zhēng</rt></ruby> <ruby>吵<rt>chǎo</rt></ruby>， <ruby>一<rt>yí</rt></ruby> <ruby>会<rt>huì</rt></ruby> <ruby>儿<rt>er</rt></ruby> <ruby>和<rt>hé</rt></ruby> <ruby>好<rt>hǎo</rt></ruby>。

<ruby>短<rt>Duǎn</rt></ruby> <ruby>暂<rt>zàn</rt></ruby> <ruby>的<rt>de</rt></ruby> <ruby>童<rt>tóng</rt></ruby> <ruby>年<rt>nián</rt></ruby>， <ruby>要<rt>yào</rt></ruby> <ruby>珍<rt>zhēn</rt></ruby> <ruby>惜<rt>xī</rt></ruby> <ruby>每<rt>měi</rt></ruby> <ruby>一<rt>yì</rt></ruby> <ruby>分<rt>fēn</rt></ruby>， <ruby>每<rt>měi</rt></ruby> <ruby>一<rt>yì</rt></ruby> <ruby>秒<rt>miǎo</rt></ruby>。

Daddy always has my back, and he makes my world so bright;
Mommy always has my heart, and she makes sure
"Everything is going to be alright!"

Sisters are always side by side, even sometimes we may fight.

CHILDHOOD is the best part of my life,
as we walk hand in hand, grin with delight.

Xiǎo xiǎo de xìng fú
小小的幸福，
yǒu nǐ men zài shēn biān
有你们在身边，
yì qǐ xiào   yì qǐ nào
一起笑，一起闹！

Every day is a **fun** day,
together with you,
my little **FAMILY**.

作者　Author

温甘玉芬

当妈前，她是孩子们的甘老师，在常年暖和的热带雨林，与孩子一起学习中、英文，探索文字的奥秘；当妈后，她是孩子们的温妈咪，在四季分明的北半球，与孩子一起感受春夏秋冬的更替，一起寻找美好的童年……

温妈咪创作的灵感，源自于多年来的童言童语。2021年，她成立了"温室工作坊"，出版一系列的中、英双语绘本，结合母语和第二语言，提倡亲子趣读。

精通三语的温妈咪理解每一种语言都有独特的艺术形式，因此她创作的双语绘本也各含韵味、各具特色。

Andrea Voon

Over the past few years, Andrea has learned and grown with her family as a full-time mother in Canada. Back in Malaysia, she worked as a teacher in Chinese immersion elementary school. In 2021, Andrea started her journey as a self-publisher. Growing up in a multilingual environment, Andrea loves the beauty of languages on their own. She has the vision to publish picture books to support bilingual families in raising their children in English and Chinese reading.

To Derek, Eliana, Alayna & Magnus Dominus
with love -- Andrea V.

绘图员

Illustrator

叶承恩

身为一名经验丰富的平面设计师和插画家，他以生动的画风，为读者带来活泼的温室一家。

Yapp Shin Enn

Shin is a graphic designer and illustrator, rich with years of experience and works with various clients. His versatile and adaptability allow him to flip the switch to meet the styles for different occasions.

BILINGUAL READING IS FUN!

Check out other bilingual picture books by Andrea Voon.

10 Chapters of teaching and learning videos in Mandarin,
include **Slow Reading, Fun Reading** and **Sing Along**
are available at
温室工作坊 Greenhouse Studio's channel
https://www.youtube.com/@greenhousestudio5929

ISBN 978-1-998856-13-8

温室工作坊

www.ingramcontent.com/pod-product-compliance
Lightning Source LLC
Chambersburg PA
CBHW041620120626
46551CB00003B/520